Made
Whole

A Guide for Achieving Financial Success

by

Eva K. Morgan

Table of contents

Introduction

Welcome to the journey of financial wholeness, which goes beyond simple wealth accumulation to explore the art of balancing your financial security with your personal goals and values. We'll examine the essence of being financially whole in this brief guide, providing helpful tips and considerate methods to assist you on your journey to a more contented and balanced financial life. Let's go on this journey together, whether you're just starting out or looking to improve your financial techniques. Along the way, success will be determined not only by numbers but also by how well your financial objectives align with the kind of life you want to lead. Greetings and welcome to the journey towards achieving financial wholeness.

Chapter 1

Adopt a financial Mindset.

Your financial mentality determines how you think about money and affects how you spend, save, and handle debt. It's your attitude toward money and your underlying thoughts about it.

This comprises:

- What do you believe you can and can't accomplish financially.
- How much you believe you should be paid.
- How you think you ought to handle your finances (spent, saved, shared).
- How you think you ought to handle your debt.
- Your capacity to increase your riches.
- Your general assurance about finances.

Mindset differences: plenty vs scarcity

Comparing plenty and scarcity mindsets to positive and negative money mindsets is another way to conceptualize them.

An attitude of scarcity manifests as:

- surviving paycheck to paycheck.
- Being overburdened, unhappy, or uninterested in your money.
- regretting previous financial errors.
- Envious of others' money management skills or outward appearance of affluence Sad about your financial circumstances.
- Resources (money, opportunity, employment, etc.) are few.
- Existing in the now because you don't think you have a long-term solution.
- It's time to change your perspective from scarcity to plenty if any of the indicators above speak to you. (It is feasible!).

Develop a money attitude that works.
The following five stages will help you master
your money attitude and show you how to go
from scarcity to abundance.

1. Consider your financial outlook.

It would help if you first took some time to
consider how your past has affected your present
to make any changes in your life, even financial
ones. Consider your financial experiences up to
this point:

- How did you grow up?
- What financial lessons did the grownups
  in your life impart to you?
- Which financial lessons were ingrained in
  you from an early age?
- Which parents or guardians were—savers
  or spenders?
- Did your parents or guardians have
  financial difficulties, or did they have easy
  access to it?
- What was their financial connection like?

- When you became an adult, how did you handle your finances?

Consider all the factors that have influenced your current perspective on money. However, remember that this is not the place to hold your parents responsible for your financial errors and pessimistic outlook on money. Yes, but only to a limited extent did the grownups in your life influence the way you think about money now. Please don't give them a call after this first step.

2. Have an optimistic outlook on money. Financial affirmations may help you change your attitude toward money and develop a positive money mentality. How you approach your money is greatly influenced by the words you use with yourself. Be mindful of the words you speak to yourself when:

- You get money (via a pay raise, bonus, job promotion, unexpected inheritance, etc.).

- You allocate that cash for bills, food, medical bills, transportation costs, and other necessities.
- You use that cash on what you consider to be indulgences.
- You commit a financial error.
- You converse with and spend time with nearby people.
- It's time to rewrite the script if these circumstances lead to critical self-talk. How can you talk to yourself differently to feel more positive?

3. Change your perspective to save money.
Next, pause to consider your financial objectives and ideals. These will assist you in managing your finances and developing an attitude of conserving money. Where do you picture yourself in one, five, ten, or twenty years? What matters to you? To help you remember your financial beliefs and objectives on the days when money seems tight, put them in writing.
Now that you've identified your objectives, use this chance to spell them out in detail. How do

you plan to bring them about? What actions are necessary for you to accomplish those goals? Dig down to the details to make your financial objectives seem more reachable.

4. Observe your spending

Monitoring your expenditures for at least one month is the most excellent approach to getting more financial knowledge and learning how to change your financial thinking. This involves controlling your emotions while handling your finances, saving, and spending.

When you are paid, what is your reaction?
What is your emotional state when you utilize money for costs or pay your bills?
Feelings when you spend money on others or yourself?
Which situations make you spend money?

5. Decide to alter your financial behaviours.

It's time to put in the effort and commit to altering your financial habits now that you're prepared to shift your financial thinking. This is your opportunity to get further financial management knowledge. Read about individuals who have overcome financial hardships to get inspiration. One such person is Ryan, who paid off $9,200 by adopting a different financial perspective. Commit to educating yourself about money using books, podcasts, blogs, online courses, workbooks, videos, and other tools so that you can change the way you think about it. How can you make a new budget that aligns with your revised perspective? What actions must you take to put your new financial strategy into practice?

Chapter 2

Make budgeting your priority.

A plan for every dollar you have is a budget. It's not magical, but it means a life free from worry and more financial independence.
Putting your monthly spending down in writing is what's known as a budget.
Maintaining a monthly income is made easier with the use of a budget. Your next paycheck might be delayed if you need more money.

A budget aids in decision-making:

What you need to buy if you can cut costs on certain items while increasing costs on others For instance, your budget may indicate you spend $200 monthly on clothing. You may determine that you have $100 to spend on clothing. The remaining funds might be saved for other goals or used to pay expenses. Creating a budget is one of the most significant ways to know where your money goes each month and what adjustments you may make to help you attain your financial objectives.

Making a budget may be done in several ways, and the best strategy for you will rely on your priorities, tastes, and objectives. You can take these actions to ensure your budget aligns with your financial objectives and way of life.

1. Establish Your Income
This first step is simple if you are paid monthly or twice a month since you are paid the same amount each month. If you get a weekly or bimonthly salary, you could make more money in some months than others. If so, you may modify your monthly budget according to the number of paychecks you anticipate receiving. Determine your typical income over the last three to six months if you work for yourself or if

your pay varies often. Since your take-home pay ends up in your bank account, please pay attention to it rather than your gross (pre-tax) income.

2. Determine Your Monthly Spending

Once you are aware of your revenue, calculate your costs similarly.
Review your credit card and bank statements from the previous three to six months to get a sense of your monthly spending patterns.

Next, divide those costs into groups, such as spending on needs vs discretionary items:

- Essentials: You have complete control over how many or how few categories you establish. For instance, you may combine regular monthly expenses like rent, utilities, and insurance or separate them into several categories. Additionally, make an effort to budget for non-recurring monthly costs like insurance premiums, tax payments, and vehicle registration renewals.

- Discretionary expenditure: It could be best to provide a more thorough breakdown of your categories when it comes to discretionary spending. Since entertainment and dining out don't always go hand in hand, you can figure out each price separately.

The more thorough your spending categories are, the simpler it will be to comprehend where your money is going and how to handle it more effectively. Keeping track of each category might also become more difficult and complex with time. Discover a healthy balance that you can maintain to be productive and motivated.

3. Make sensible objectives
After you have an understanding of your spending patterns, take some time to plan your future financial objectives.

For instance, decide how much you'll pay each month if you want to pay off your debt more quickly. Then, ensure it occurs by setting objectives to reduce expenditure in certain areas. It's important to have lofty yet attainable objectives. If your expectations are too high, it may be hard to maintain your motivation when things don't go your way.

Establish SMART (specific, measurable, attainable, reasonable, and timely) objectives that may push you a little, but remember that creating the habits you want to have might take some time. Even with data supporting your estimates, it's simple to underestimate certain costs. As you get used to the procedure, make modifications in light of your budget's realities.

4. Monitor Your Expenses
It's one thing to monitor your income and make financial objectives, but it will only help a little if you also monitor your expenditures.
It will not be difficult challenging to track your spending, mainly if you often make many transactions daily. The procedure may get

complicated if cash, debit, and credit cards are combined.

To help in the process, consider utilizing budgeting tools like Mint, or You Need a Budget. These applications may integrate your revenue and transactions into one location by connecting to your bank accounts, making managing and classifying every spending simpler.
Apart from providing an extra measure of responsibility, monitoring your expenses may assist you in validating your hypotheses and objectives and guide you on how to modify them in subsequent months.

5. Select a Spending Scheme
Now that you understand the fundamentals, it's time to consider if you want to adopt a particular budgeting plan in addition to the previously covered ones.
Consider how each budgeting strategy aligns with your money management style as you read

about it, then choose the one you believe will work best for you.

Here are four popular budgeting techniques to think about.

- Envelope system: In this traditional method, you set aside a certain amount of money for each expenditure category and place that money in an envelope labelled with the category's name. You need to transfer money from another envelope to run out of funds for that category for the remainder of the month after you've used up all the cash in that envelope.
- 50/30/20 schedule: 50% of your take-home salary should go into essentials like housing, utilities, and auto payments; 30% should go toward discretionary spending; and 20% should go toward your financial objectives, which include debt repayment and savings. This is known as the 50/30/20 budget. Depending on your

circumstances, you may modify the proportions to meet your demands and objectives.

- Two-account plan: In this approach, your monthly fixed costs are totaled and divided by the number of paychecks you get. When paid, put that fixed-expense amount into one bank account and the remaining amount into another for discretionary expenditure.
- Zero-based spending strategy: The goal of a zero-based budget is to give each dollar a purpose, so your out-of-pocket spending should match your take-home income. With this degree of detail, you can see exactly where your money is going, but maintain a healthy emergency fund in case your expenses increase or you incur a big one.

6. Adhere to Your Budget

The most superficial aspect of budgeting is coming up with a budget. The problem is frequently remembering to monitor and restrict your monthly spending to stay within your budget. The following advice will help you stick to your budget:

- Be sensible. Once again, creating realistic objectives is essential since doing so keeps you from falling short. This is particularly crucial when you're just getting started and need all the inspiration you can muster.
- Make advance plans. Life will almost certainly go differently than planned. Therefore, it's critical to have emergency reserves on hand. Remember that not all recurring costs occur every month. Make sure to budget for any costs that you have that happen on a quarterly or yearly basis, such as Christmas shopping and transportation expenses.

- Be adaptable. Allow for some flexibility to adjust your life; therefore, your spending changes over time. A few costs might make everything go right if your budget is flexible.
- When necessary, turn around. Be bold and modify your strategy if your budget isn't helping you manage your money as well as it might or if your objectives or financial circumstances have changed.
- Make responsible use of credit cards. If you do not want to, you are not required to use credit cards. However, if you do, you must use your credit cards sensibly. Keeping track of your spending can help you stick to your spending plan. Ideally, minimizing late payments and debt growth entails maintaining modest amounts and making whole monthly payments.

Above All, Never Forget Your Objectives

Creating a budget is a significant first step in the right direction. It will show you where your money is going and where you can cut down on spending to free up funds for a house, a vehicle, or other financial objectives.
But it could be more enjoyable to budget just for budgeting. Remind yourself of the reasons for your monthly budget while you work with it. Additionally, frequently assess your progress to ensure that you are on course to reach your objectives.

Chapter 3

Pay off your debt.

Financial difficulty may result from having excessive debt in several ways. It might be tough to make ends meet, or your credit can worsen, making it harder to get approved for further loans like mortgages or vehicle loans.

You may take many actions to clear your debt and start on a sound financial path if you're carrying a significant amount of debt.

1. Enumerate All of Your Debts

To clearly understand your current situation, do a thorough inventory of all of your debt. List all of your debt accounts along with the total amount you owe first:

- Put all of your debts on paper. Make a list of everything you owe, including the amounts on your credit cards, personal and vehicle loans, school loans, mortgages, and other debt. If you want a thorough picture of your obligations, including those in collections, check your credit report for free to figure out what you owe. Remember that your lender can access the most recent information on your balances.

- Keep track of payment details. Note the interest rate, minimum monthly payment, and due date next to each obligation.
- Determine the total amount that you must pay each month. To determine the bare minimum you must pay monthly to remain current on your debt, add up the minimum payments for all your bills.

2. Determine Your Monthly Payment Cap
Making all your minimum monthly payments on your debts will result in longer repayment terms and higher interest rates, but it will also maintain a positive payment history. You may pay off debt more quickly if you pay more than the minimum monthly.

But it can be easier said than done when finances are tight. Here are some tips for determining how much you can afford to pay each month and how to locate additional funds to apply to your debt:

- Determine how much you'll be spending each month. Determine how much you spend each month on necessities like food, your phone bill, electricity, petrol for your vehicle, rent or mortgage payments, and so on by using a spreadsheet or a budgeting tool. Consider averaging your monthly power bill or other variable costs over many months.
- Evaluate your income and spending. Add up your monthly net income, which is your after-tax take-home pay. Deduct all of your out-of-pocket costs from your monthly income, considering both mandatory and optional costs like entertainment and other non-essential spending. If the remaining amount is insufficient to assist in paying off your debt, you'll need to change your spending

or source of income to boost your cash flow.

- Seek chances to make savings. Examine every penny you spend and think of methods to save, including reducing eating out and shopping at stores or haggling over utilities and other services.
- Boost or add to your revenue. You can earn more money to pay off your debts by starting a side business, working longer hours, or requesting a raise.

3. Lower Your Loan Amounts

Debt repayment might be challenging if you're up against hefty interest rates. Lowering your rates is an excellent way to make debt repayment more inexpensive and doable. Think about any of the following:

- Request a cheaper rate from your lender. You can work out a temporary or permanent reduced rate with your lender if you have a solid payment history and strong credit. It doesn't cost you anything to call your lender and request a lower interest rate, and it has no impact on your credit score or report.

- Check out a credit card that transfers balances. Using a balance transfer card with an initial 0% APR is one option to transfer balances and save money while you pay off your debt. You must fulfil the requirements set out by the balance transfer card issuer, including having excellent credit and a transfer charge of 3% or 5% of your transfer amount.

- Think about consolidating your debt. By consolidating many high-interest credit card or loan amounts into a single, lower-interest loan, a debt consolidation loan may help you save money on interest and simplify debt payments. It could be simpler to contribute more money to the principal reduction of the loan if interest costs are decreased.

4. Employ a Plan for Paying Off Debt

You'll need to decide which amounts should be paid off first in priority. Remember that your mortgage is one item you may not be able to pay off quickly; instead, concentrate on debts you can pay off more quickly, such credit card amounts and other loans. Take a look at these methods for debt repayment:

- Take care of any outstanding bills. Make paying off your debt a top priority if you need to catch up on payments, and it's now in collections. It would help if you prioritized paying off collection accounts as soon as possible since doing so may lessen the harm they inflict on your credit. Additionally, cutting down on debt collection calls might help lessen the stress associated with having debt.
- Add more funds to the obligation whose interest rate is greater. This approach, the debt avalanche plan, will result in the

most long-term interest cost savings. After paying the minimum amount owed on each loan, apply any remaining funds to the obligation with the highest interest rate. Focus on the debt with the next-highest interest rate after that, and so on.

- Add more funds to the loan or credit card with the lowest balance. With the debt snowball plan, you may reduce the number of accounts you have to manage and get immediate victories by paying off your smaller sums first. Using this approach, you pay the minimal amount due on each account and use additional funds to pay down your lowest debt. Next, concentrate on the next-to-smallest account amount, and so on.

- Put the money you free up toward paying off your other bills each time you pay off a loan. Additionally, you may use any additional money you receive—like a job bonus or tax refund—to pay off your debt faster.

When you reduce your debt, remember your credit. Paying your payments on time each month is one of the finest things you can do to improve your credit score. It would help if you thought consider establishing automated payments or payment reminders via your bank to ensure you never forget to pay for debts or any other services.

5. Refrain from Accruing New Debt
Paying off debt takes a lot of work. Celebrate your accomplishments and feel proud as you get closer to paying off your obligations.

Make a promise to only take on further debt once it is essential. If you want to utilize a balance transfer card or personal loan to pay off credit card debt, proceed with extra caution. It's better to avoid combining your debt if you don't think you can withstand the urge to charge up the cards you just paid off.

What to Do in Case You Still Require
Assistance in Paying Off Debt

Finding oneself deeply in debt may be stressful,
mainly if there is no way out. Take into account
these steps whether you need further assistance
or are searching for a last-resort solution:

- Credit counselling: Speaking with a
  nonprofit credit counsellor may help you
  comprehend budgeting and debt reduction
  strategies, such as making and sticking to
  a spending plan.
- Debt management plan: If you are deeply
  in debt, especially with credit cards, a
  credit counselling group may recommend
  a debt management plan. This kind of plan
  is intended to assist you in managing your
  payback. A credit counsellor works with
  your creditors to work out lower interest
  rates, more manageable monthly
  payments, or even the waiver of some
  costs. After that, you make a monthly
  payment to the credit counselling firm,

which disburses the money to your creditors per your arrangement.

- One of the most critical steps toward long-term financial stability is paying off high-interest debt. You may take several self-help measures to take charge of your debt, including creating a budget, adhering to a repayment plan, and consolidating your loans. A credit counsellor may assist you in creating a plan that is specific to your financial situation if you want extra assistance.

- You may start repairing your credit after you've decreased or even paid off your debt by using sound credit and money management techniques. Pay your payments on schedule, and refrain from carrying a monthly balance on your credit card.

Chapter 4

Discovering ways to raise your income

If you are looking for ways to raise your income and would like to know how to do so? You may save, invest, and pay off your debts more quickly if your income increases. It may expedite the time it takes you to reach your financial objectives far more quickly than if your only emphasis was on cutting costs.

Still, many believe that boosting your income is a challenging task. It doesn't have to be, however! Now, let's talk about ways to make additional money quickly.

Eight strategies to boost your income
Here are eight straightforward strategies to effectively increase revenue that you can put into practice right now:

1. Request an increase or bonus
When did you most recently request a raise at work? Or do you wait to get one? One of the best ways to quickly boost your income is to ask for a raise.

However, you must ensure that you do it correctly. When preparing to ask your supervisor for a raise, you must be ready for the talk. Keep a record of your professional achievements and honours. Ensure to emphasize certain measurements and results to demonstrate how your efforts and skill set have favourably impacted the company's ability to achieve its goals. Put simply, you'll have to sell your story with enthusiasm.

Don't give up if you can't get a raise right away. Ask your manager to find out what it takes to get your next job bonus or increase.

2. Find a higher-paying job

Is a raise now out of the question? Was the increase you got just insufficient? Now is the right moment to update your LinkedIn profile and CV in preparation for a higher-paying position.

Before you apply for employment, you can use a website like Glassdoor to investigate wages in your area. This will give you a fair indication of what you should be paid. Additionally, you can consider enrolling in classes or obtaining qualifications that would enable you to earn more money.

3. Take up a side job.

If your schedule allows, part-time work might be a terrific way to increase your income. particularly if a better-paying position or a raise is not readily accessible. Your part-time work can be something other than a permanent or elaborate position.

You may work part-time until you reach a certain amount of money or for a certain period. It all comes down to concentrating on your goals and leveraging part-time work to help you reach them more quickly.

You must pay close attention to how you spend the additional money you make from part-time employment.

The last thing you want is to work longer hours and sacrifice more time for your family or yourself to make ends meet, only to have the money escape your grasp.

4. Launch a cheap side business.

The best way to boost your income while developing a company is to start a side gig. It enables you to make money from your skills or interests. You may start your side business on the weekends or evenings after work.

Popular sectors in which to launch a side business include:

- Fitness, wellness, and health, such as food preparation, personal training, coaching, and leading a healthy lifestyle
- Fashion and beauty, such as style and product reviews
- Technology assistance, such as website development, graphic design, and social media management
- Blogging, such as posting often on a specialized subject and making use of partnerships and affiliate connections,
- Events such as weddings, business gatherings, celebrations, and lifestyle shots
- Food-related jobs include baking, catering, instructing workshops, and making useful films.

Remember that you must exercise patience to expand your side project to a profitable level. Additionally, you may need specialized business knowledge in areas like marketing, finance, and company planning.

5. Sort through your belongings and sell them
These days, we tend to buy more items than we need. Because of this, we sometimes acquire more than we need, and many unnecessary items clog up our houses.

It's a terrific idea to declutter if you're experiencing this. You may make some additional money by selling items you no longer need but still have value.

The influence this money may have on reaching your financial objectives is substantial. Etsy, eBay, Poshmark, Facebook Marketplace, and Etsy are some places you may sell fast.

6. Reduce costs wherever you can
You may be surprised at how much money you might lose on hidden costs like excessive energy bills, squandered food, and unused subscriptions. To increase revenue rapidly, look for methods to reduce spending and your budget.

For example, consider these tips for cutting your electricity costs, comparing insurance quotes, and preparing your meals in advance to avoid ordering takeout when you're not in the mood to cook.

If your weekly dining-out expenses are $50, it comes to $2,600 a year! That may be used for a pleasant family trip or added to your emergency fund. Reducing spending is a clever method of generating more revenue!

7. Turn your hobbies into cash

One way to boost your income while having fun is to turn your interests into a business! If you prefer to DIY, you may sell the cute things you produce on websites like Etsy. Alternatively, you may sell flowers and plants at your neighbourhood farmer's market if you're a green thumb.

You may earn money from your hobby! One of the best ways to increase revenue rapidly is to use the activities you like.

8. Generate a side source of income

One way to consistently get additional money is through passive income. The nice part about passive income is that you can keep making money from it even after doing the initial setup or labour.

Among the many methods to generate passive income include stock market investments, book royalties, and rental property income.

Knowing the distinction between active and passive income is a good concept. Hence, passive income is what you make long after the task is done, but active income is what you "actively" work at a side project or employment.

Ensure you have the correct goals for your extra money when you go above and beyond to boost your revenue. You want to save time and additional income after working so hard to get that money.

Make making a plan ahead of time a priority to pay off your debt, save more money, invest more, and achieve your other objectives.

Chapter 5

Make retirement investments.

The process of preparing for retirement involves several steps that change over time. It would help if you accumulated the necessary financial cushion to have a safe, enjoyable, and happy retirement. Planning your route is the important and dull portion, but it makes sense to focus on it since it's the exciting part.

The first step in retirement planning is determining your retirement objectives and the time frame they must meet. Next, consider the types of retirement accounts that may assist you in raising the capital required to finance your future. You must make investments with the money you save for it to increase.

Taxes are the last component of planning; if you have accumulated tax deductions for your retirement account contributions throughout the years, you will face a significant tax bill when you begin to take those assets. When you prepare for the future and when the time comes to quitting working, there are strategies to reduce the retirement tax bite.

Here, we'll discuss each of these concerns. But first, regardless of age, begin by understanding the five steps everyone should follow to create a strong retirement plan.

For retirement, how much money do you need to save?

Someone has to have a solid understanding of how much money they need to save before they can begin crunching the numbers on their retirement objectives. Their yearly salary and the age at which they want to retire are only two examples of the many situational considerations that will inevitably affect this.

Although there isn't a set amount of money that must be saved, many retirement experts suggest starting with a savings of around $1 million, or 12 years' worth of annual income before retirement. Some advocate for the 4% rule, which states that pensioners should spend no more than 4% of their retirement assets annually to guarantee a good retirement.

Since every person's position is unique, it is worthwhile to take some time to determine how much money you should save for retirement.

Things to Take Into Account
Consider a few variables that may impact your retirement objectives when you start to think about retiring. As an example, what are your family's plans? Although establishing a family is a top priority for many individuals, having kids may also significantly reduce your finances. Your retirement planning will thus consider your desired family structure.

Similarly, considering your retirement plans, including any modifications to your house or living place, is good. While extended travel might be a great experience, it can deplete your retirement assets more quickly than remaining at home, even though many individuals dream of travelling throughout their retirement. However, relocating to a nation with a very low cost of living can help you stretch your funds further while still enjoying a good level of life. Lastly, it's important to consider the various kinds of tax-advantaged retirement funds. Most Americans are eligible for social security payments, yet they seldom cover all their retirement costs.

Following careful consideration of these variables, you should take the following actions to begin retirement planning:

1. Recognize your time frame
The foundation of a successful retirement plan is laid by your present age and anticipated retirement age. Your portfolio can tolerate a

greater risk the longer you retire. Should you be young and have more than 30 years before retiring, you may allocate the bulk of your assets to riskier investments like equities. Although there may be volatility, stocks have generally done better over extended periods than other products, such as bonds. "Long" is the keyword here, indicating a minimum of ten years.
It would help if you also had returns that exceeded inflation to keep your buying power in retirement.

Income and capital preservation should make up a larger portion of your portfolio as you age. This entails investing a larger portion of your portfolio in safer assets like bonds, which won't provide the same returns as equities but will be less volatile and provide you with a living wage. Additionally, you won't be as concerned about inflation. The concerns about rising living expenses are not the same for a 64-year-old who intends to retire next year as they are for a much younger professional who has just started working.

2. Establish Needs for Retirement Spending

You may determine the necessary size of a retirement portfolio by setting reasonable expectations for your post-retirement spending patterns. Most respondents think their yearly expenditure after retirement will only be between 70% and 80% of what they did before.

This kind of assumption is often shown to be unrealistic, particularly in cases where the mortgage has yet to be paid off or when unanticipated medical costs arise. Sometimes, after retirement, individuals indulge in travel or other lifelong dreams during their initial retirement years.

"I think the ratio should be closer to 100% for retired adults to have enough savings for retirement," states David G. Niggel, CFP, ChFC, AIF, founder, president, and CEO of Key Wealth Partners LLC in Lititz, Pennsylvania.

"Every year, living costs rise, particularly those related to healthcare. People want to enjoy their retirement years and are living longer. Retired adults need to earn more money for longer, so they must invest and save appropriately.

3. Determine the Investment return After-Tax Rate
To evaluate whether the portfolio can provide the required income, the after-tax real rate of return must be computed after the projected time horizons and expenditure needs have been established. Even for long-term investment, a needed rate of return above 10% (before taxes) is often an unreasonable expectation. This return requirement decreases with age since low-risk retirement portfolios mostly comprise fixed-income investments with low yields.

For instance, if a person's retirement portfolio is worth $400,000 and their income requirements are $50,000—assumed tax-free, and the portfolio balance is preserved—they depend on an unsustainable 12.5% return to make ends meet. Growing the portfolio to ensure a reasonable rate of return is one of the main benefits of starting retirement planning early. With a $1 million gross retirement investment account, the predicted return would be a much more realistic 5%.

Depending on the type of retirement account that you hold, investment returns are typically taxed. Therefore, the actual rate of return must be calculated on an after-tax basis. However, determining your tax status when you withdraw funds is crucial to the retirement planning process.

4. Evaluate Investment Objectives vs. Risk Tolerance

The most crucial stage in retirement planning is creating a suitable portfolio allocation that balances risk aversion and return targets, whether you or a professional money manager are in charge of making the investment selections. To what extent are you prepared to take risks to achieve your goals? Should a portion of income be invested in risk-free Treasury bonds to cover necessary expenses?

5. Continue to Monitor Estate Planning

Another crucial component of a comprehensive retirement plan is estate planning, each of which calls for the knowledge of specialized experts in their respective fields, such as accountants and attorneys. A life insurance policy is also a crucial component of retirement and estate planning. It's important to have life insurance and an appropriate estate plan to ensure your assets are disbursed according to your wishes and that your loved ones won't face financial difficulties when you pass away. A well-thought-out plan also helps prevent a costly and often drawn-out probate procedure.

Chapter 6

Selecting the Right Financial Advisor

For every budget and financial circumstance, there is a financial counsellor. This chapter explains the many kinds of financial advisers and how to choose the best one for you.

Financial advisers assist clients in budgeting and achieving their financial objectives. They may provide various financial planning services, including investment management, money management, and advice on creating a budget. Certain financial advisers can assist with intricate financial matters like estate planning, insurance requirements, or tax preparation because they possess extra credentials or areas of specialization.

Choosing the best financial adviser for your circumstances is important since doing so will save you from paying for unnecessary services or dealing with an advisor who matches your financial objectives differently. To assist you in selecting a financial adviser, consider the following five steps:

1. Determine what you need financially. Consider what you want from that connection before searching for the perfect counsel. Knowing what you need assistance with before you start your search is a smart idea,, since financial advisers provide various services. While some advisers may provide comprehensive assistance, advising you on everything from savings objectives to retirement and estate planning, others may specialize in certain areas of finance, such as debt management or investing guidance.

Asking yourself the following questions can help you determine why you need financial assistance:

- Need assistance creating a budget?

- Would you want assistance with investing?

- Do you want to put up a budget?

- Do you need assistance achieving any savings objectives?

- Do you need to set up a trust or organize your estate plan?

- Do you need assistance with taxes?

- Do you have any interest in comprehensive money management?

You can identify the best kind of financial counsellor for you by answering these questions. Additionally, it could assist you in determining whether you need one. For example, a robo-advisor may invest for you for a little charge if all you want help with is investing. On the other hand, you could look for an online or conventional financial counsellor if you have a complicated financial life with several financial issues you want to address.

2: Recognize the different kinds of financial counsellors.
There are several titles for financial advisers, including investment advisor, portfolio manager, financial coach, professional financial planner, and broker. Even financial therapists exist. Don't assume that someone who uses an official-sounding title has any particular training or qualifications since some of the most frequently used titles by advisers, such as "financial advisor," aren't associated with any particular credentials.

Who can you trust, and who does what? To ensure you're dealing with someone with your best interests in mind, there are a few techniques to get beyond the crowd.

- Fiduciary financial advisers who take fees solely

Certain financial advisers must operate in their customers' best interests rather than their own since they owe them a fiduciary obligation. Dealing with a duly registered and licensed fiduciary—ideally one that charges a flat fee— guarantees that you will pay the adviser directly rather than via commissions for the sale of specific investment or insurance products.

As part of their accreditation, financial advisers with the Certified Financial Planner (CFP) title owe their customers a fiduciary obligation.

- Financial advisors

Depending on how many assets they handle, individuals who provide financial advice must register as investment advisors with the state or the U.S. Securities and Exchange Commission. Investment consultants employed by firms or individuals may function as registered investment advisors, or RIAs.

3.Examine the variety of financial adviser alternatives available.

You may find financial advisers at places other than your local bank or advising office. Getting financial guidance may be done in a variety of ways. Your budget, the services you need, and your tastes will probably determine which choice is best for you. Below is a summary of the various service categories, which include high-touch, conventional financial advisers and low-cost computerized robo-advisors:

- Artificial Advisors

A robo-advisor is an online platform that provides affordable, streamlined financial management. After you respond to online questionnaires, computer algorithms create an investing portfolio based on your objectives and risk tolerance.

- Low cost: You may start investing with any amount of money since many robo-advisors have no or low account minimums, and others offer no management fees.

4. Think about the amount you can afford to pay a consultant.

Although they have a reputation for being expensive, financial advisers are available for any budget. Before hiring a financial adviser, knowing how much their services will cost is critical. In general, you'll probably come across three different pricing levels:

A yearly fee, often calculated as a percentage of your account balance, is levied by robo-advisors. The starting price for a robo-advisor is often 0.25% of the assets they manage on your behalf; however, many of the best firms charge as little as 0.50%. 0.25% of a $50,000 account balance is $125 annually.

Online advisers and services for financial planning usually charge a portion of your assets, a fixed membership fee, or both. Empower, for instance, levies annual fees ranging from 0.49% to 0.89% of assets under management. Facet levies an annual fee that increases according to the intricacy of your financial circumstances, starting at $2,000. Financial planning and portfolio management are included in both costs.

With a typical cost of 1%, traditional financial advisers also often charge a proportion of the managed assets; however, this fee might vary depending on the account size. Some could bill by the hour, by the flat price, or by a retainer.

Your budget, assets, and the extent of financial advice you need will determine how much you should spend on a financial adviser. An in-person adviser may be unnecessary if your portfolio is modest; a robo-advisor may help you save money and yet provide the necessary recommendations. A robo-advisor might not be the right solution if your financial situation is complex.

Examine the history of the financial adviser. It is your responsibility to verify the qualifications and expertise of the adviser, regardless of any title, distinction, certification, or license they may claim to have. Always confirm the legitimacy of their credentials and inquire about past disciplinary issues, such as fraud.

Chapter 7

Make a lasting legacy

You work all of your life to make sure you can support your family's needs as well as your own. After you reach that threshold, it might be time to think about the kind of financial legacy you want to leave your loved ones.

Why Is It Important to Leave a Financial Legacy?

There is so much more to the legacy you leave with your family than just material possessions. Relationships are defined by the lessons learned; the laughs shared the support, and the love. Giving the next generation the resources they need to succeed is the goal. Therefore, even though it's not the only way to leave a legacy, money can still be a valuable asset for creating a future.

A financial legacy can assist your heirs in moving forward, regardless of their current financial circumstances. It could be used for starting a business, buying a house, or for education. It can also be used to honour you or strengthen the bonds between your family members by supporting a cause that's important to you or by paying for a trip. It can contribute to the accumulation of wealth that will benefit current and future generations.

You can feel more at ease knowing that the things you have worked your entire life to accumulate will benefit the people you love and care about if you know how your finances will affect the world.

Three Steps to Creating a Lasting Financial Legacy

1. Establish an Estate Plan
To begin leaving a legacy, the simplest and first step is to draft an estate plan that specifies how your belongings will be divided when you pass away. A common misperception is that having an estate plan only benefits the wealthy. In reality, though, having a smaller estate may require an estate plan more than a larger one because neglecting the plan could burden your heirs.

A legal document known as an estate plan allows you to safeguard your assets for designated loved ones. Usually, creating a will is necessary, but other estate planning instruments like trusts may also be used. Life insurance is frequently used to provide for your family's needs after you pass away, in addition to protecting them. Because you can name beneficiaries to receive the remaining financial assets after your death, retirement accounts can also be used in estate planning.

To make sure your estate plan and all of its tools are used appropriately, you should collaborate with an accountant, attorney, and financial advisor. You should review your plan on a regular basis, particularly in the event of a marriage or divorce, birth, death, change in your estate, or modification of estate laws. Reviewing the plan every three to five years is a good benchmark outside of these occasions.

2. Talk To Your Successors

When it comes to inheritances, communication is essential. Family conflicts can arise from unclear expectations not being communicated, which can lead to divergent views about the benefactor's intended use of the funds.

Discuss with your family how much and how you plan to leave them, as well as when they can expect it and how you see them using these resources. The notion that beneficiaries will depend on an inheritance windfall rather than achieving financial stability themselves is one argument against communicating this. However, keeping quiet also means that your beneficiaries will need to be made aware of your intentions and ready to accept the inheritance.

When the time comes to talk about inheritances, you should think about giving your children access to your Journal of Wishes and Records. This will help them understand your financial situation and provide guidance while they carry out your wishes.

3. Instill Financial Responsibility in Your Kids

According to research, historically, just 30% of wealth survives into the second generation, and 10% survives into the third.1. It's important to teach your children and grandchildren how to manage those funds so they can be ready for their inheritance. It can be challenging to have financial conversations, but it can be even more challenging to make wise financial decisions on your own without assistance.

It takes more than just money to leave a legacy for your family; it also involves your support and guidance on how they should continue that legacy.

Conclusion

Achieving financial success is a journey rather than a destination that calls for flexibility, awareness, and a dedication to continuous improvement. I hope the knowledge in these chapters has enabled you to make wise choices, develop a healthy relationship with money, and take calculated steps to reach your financial objectives.

Recall that building a life of plenty, security, and fulfilment is more important for reaching financial wholeness than the figures on a balance sheet. Accept the lessons you've learned and use them as stepping stones to advance yourself as you navigate your financial path.

The path to financial achievement is individual, and I hope "Made Whole" has been a trustworthy companion, providing useful resources and viewpoints to improve your financial health. Whether you're just getting started or are a seasoned investor, know that your commitment to this path demonstrates your desire for a more stable and prosperous future.

www.ingramcontent.com/pod-product-compliance
Lightning Source LLC
Chambersburg PA
CBHW062251290526
45794CB00006B/2505